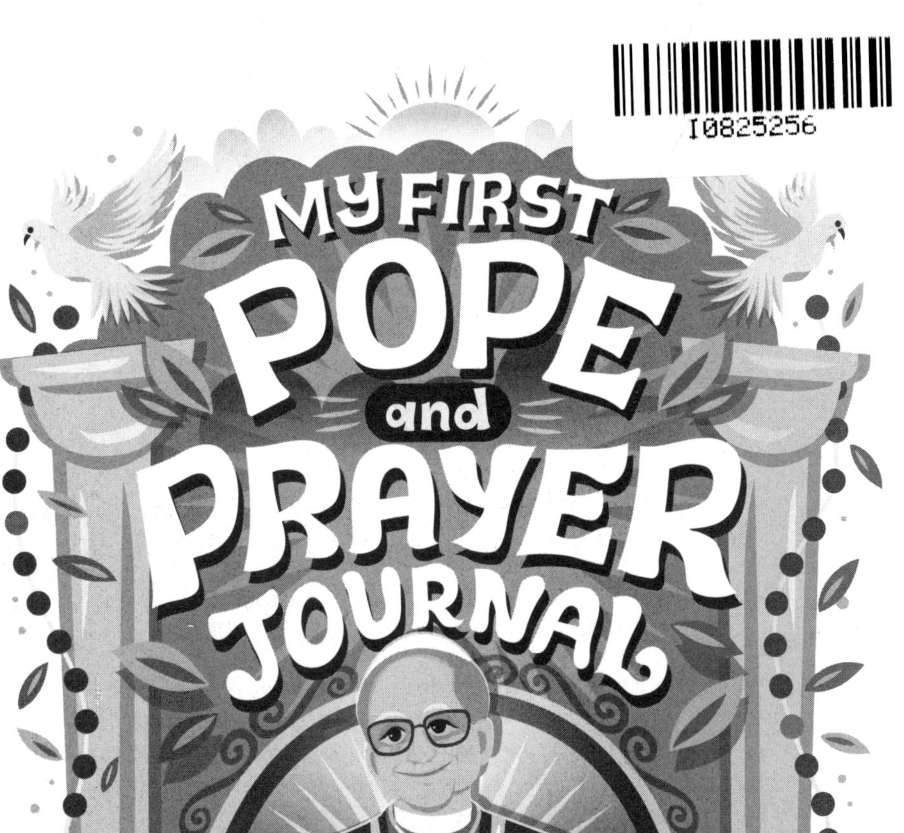

MY FIRST POPE and PRAYER JOURNAL

A FAITH GUIDE INSPIRED BY POPE LEO XIV

BY PIA IMPERIAL
ILLUSTRATED BY Risa Rodil

Grosset & Dunlap

GROSSET & DUNLAP
An imprint of Penguin Random House LLC
1745 Broadway, New York, NY 10019
penguinrandomhouse.com

Photo credits: (stained glass pattern) GreenSkyStudio/Adobe Stock, (cross pattern) ThephotoLab/Adobe Stock

Design by Kimberley Sampson

First published in the United States of America by Grosset & Dunlap, 2026

Manufactured in Canada
FRI

ISBN 9798217247172
10 9 8 7 6 5 4 3 2 1

The authorized representative in the EU for product safety and compliance is Penguin Random House Ireland, Morrison Chambers, 32 Nassau Street, Dublin D02 YH68, Ireland, https://eu-contact.penguin.ie.

TABLE OF CONTENTS

Part I

Part II

Part III

Part IV

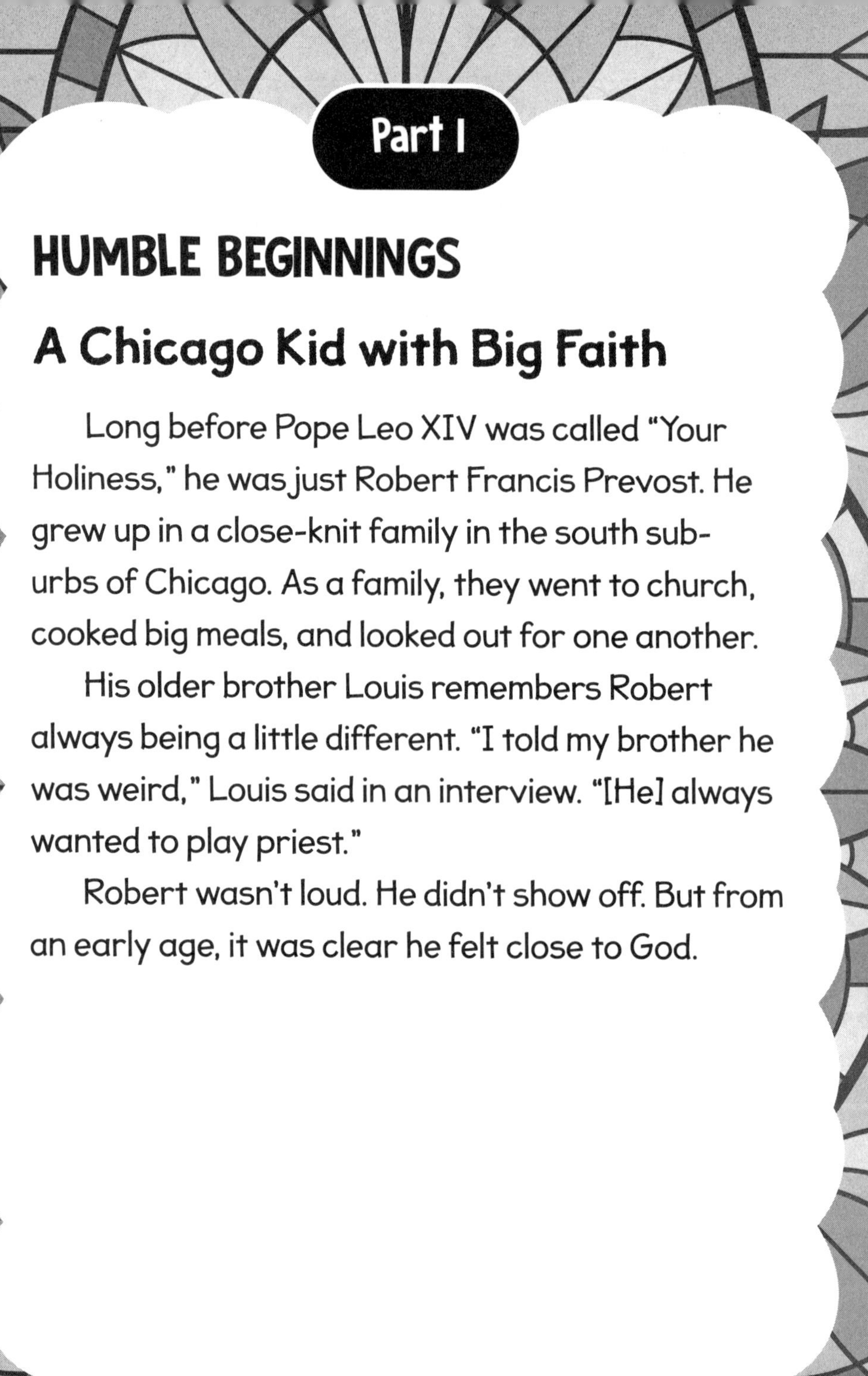

Part I

HUMBLE BEGINNINGS

A Chicago Kid with Big Faith

Long before Pope Leo XIV was called "Your Holiness," he was just Robert Francis Prevost. He grew up in a close-knit family in the south suburbs of Chicago. As a family, they went to church, cooked big meals, and looked out for one another.

His older brother Louis remembers Robert always being a little different. "I told my brother he was weird," Louis said in an interview. "[He] always wanted to play priest."

Robert wasn't loud. He didn't show off. But from an early age, it was clear he felt close to God.

Date: Su / M / Tu / W / Th / F / Sa

__ / __ / ____

Today I Feel:

Today I'm Thankful For:

1 ______________________________

____

____

____

2 ______________________________

____

____

____

3 ______________________________

____

____

____

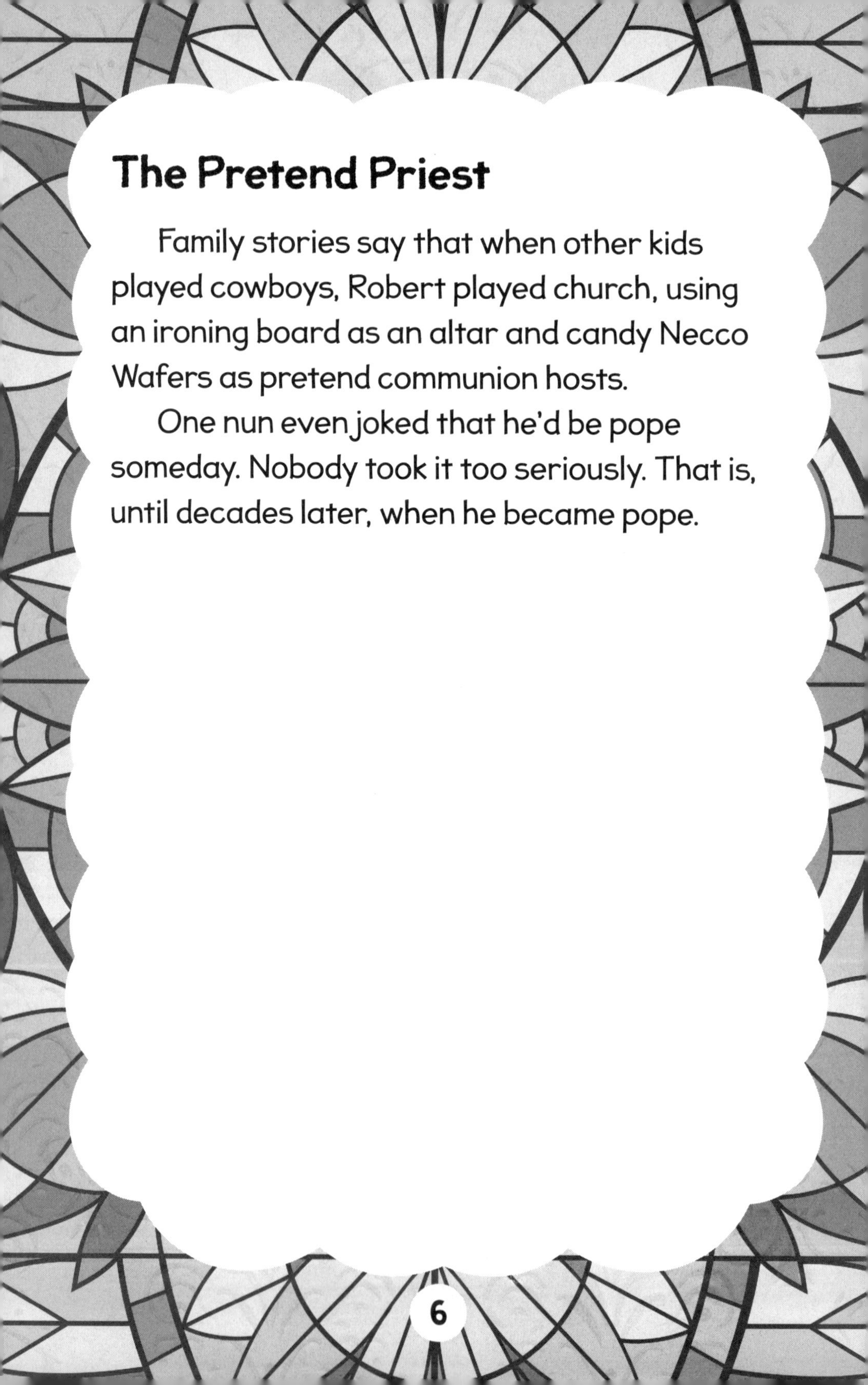

The Pretend Priest

Family stories say that when other kids played cowboys, Robert played church, using an ironing board as an altar and candy Necco Wafers as pretend communion hosts.

One nun even joked that he'd be pope someday. Nobody took it too seriously. That is, until decades later, when he became pope.

Date: Su / M / Tu / W / Th / F / Sa

__ / __ / ____

Today I Feel:

Think of someone who helped you in a small but powerful way—maybe a teacher, a friend, or a neighbor. Write them a short thank-you note here.

A Student of Faith

At school, Robert's classmates recall him being a good student who was devoted to his studies and God.

He read his Bible. He served as an altar boy and sang in the church choir. He asked big questions and then listened hard to the answers.

Even as a teenager, Robert wanted to do more than just understand his faith. He wanted to live it.

Date: Su / M / Tu / W / Th / F / Sa

__ / __ / ____

Today I Feel:

Today I'm Thankful For:

1 ______________________________

____

____

____

2 ______________________________

____

____

____

3 ______________________________

____

____

____

Leading by Listening

While serving as an altar boy, Robert wasn't the loudest voice in the room—but people listened when he spoke. He had a way of holding silence that made people lean in.

When his friends argued, he calmed things down. When someone cried, he stayed beside them. He didn't lead by shouting. He led by listening.

And that made all the difference.

Date: Su / M / Tu / W / Th / F / Sa

__ / __ / ____

Today I Feel:

Leo didn't try to impress anyone. He often just did the right thing. What's one small act of love, kindness, or service you could do this week without anyone noticing?

Leo's Lightbulbs

1 He grew up in Dolton, Illinois, just outside Chicago.

2 His family has Creole roots tracing back to Louisiana.

3 He is a fan of the Chicago White Sox.

4 He attended Game One of the 2005 World Series, between the White Sox and Astros.

5 He's a fan of puzzles.

6 He is known as "Father Bob" in Chicago.

7 He is known as "Padre Roberto" in Peru.

8 He was serious about his faith from a young age.

9 His childhood parish was St. Mary of the Assumption.

10 He later studied at Villanova University.

Quiet Strength

Some people lead with a megaphone. Others lead with a whisper.

What's one quiet thing you do that makes a big difference? It might be listening well. It might be making someone laugh. Write about a time when your quietness became your strength.

Helping Hands

Leo's story reminds us that faith doesn't always need a stage. Sometimes it just needs a helper.

Write about a time when you helped someone without being asked.

How did it feel? Did they notice? Did it matter?

Where You're From

Leo carried his Chicago roots with him all the way to Rome. He never forgot where he came from.

What do you love most about where you're from? Write about your neighborhood, family, or traditions. What do they teach you?

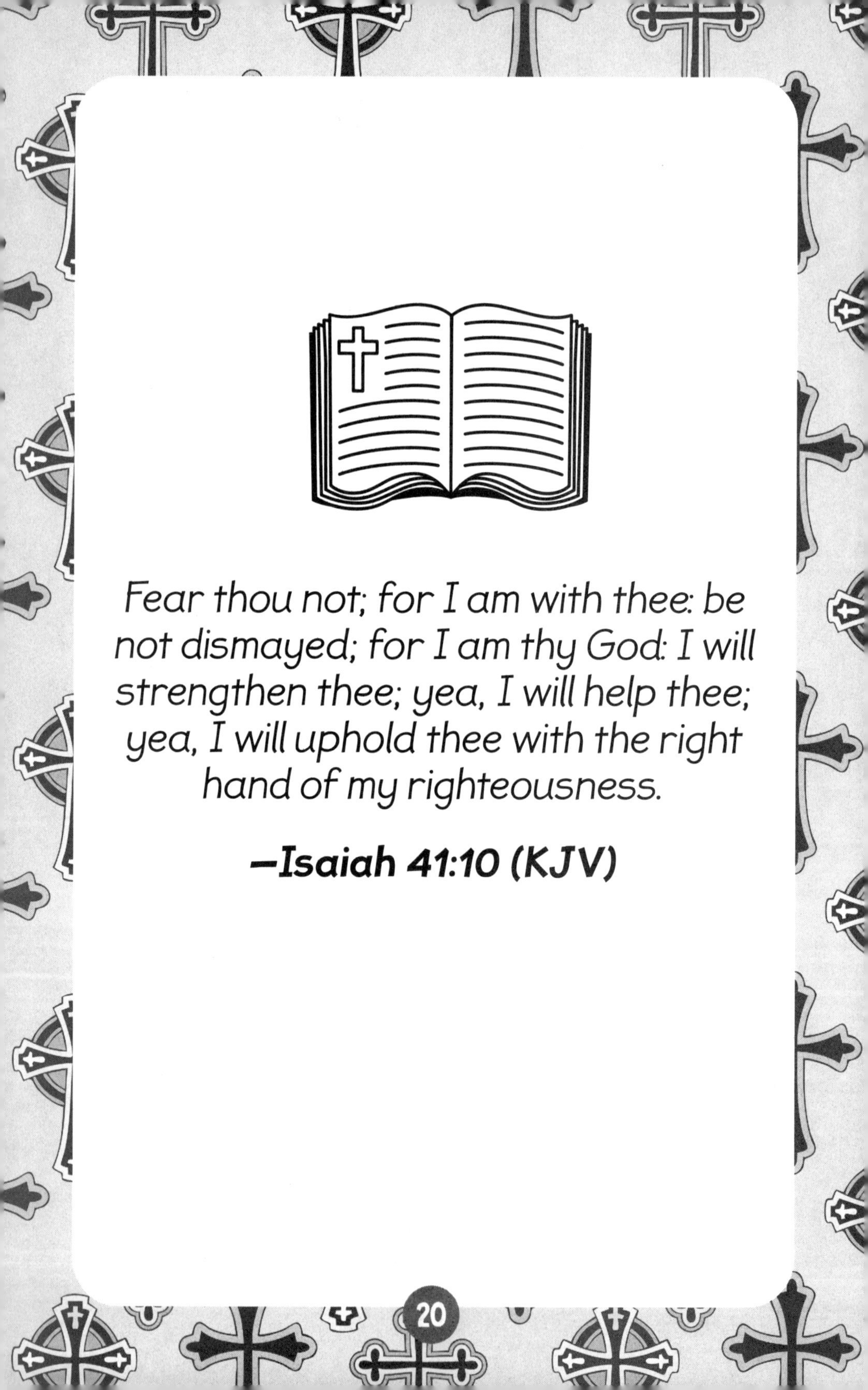

Fear thou not; for I am with thee: be not dismayed; for I am thy God: I will strengthen thee; yea, I will help thee; yea, I will uphold thee with the right hand of my righteousness.

—Isaiah 41:10 (KJV)

Which people in your life are always there to support you? Write them a thank-you note.

Date: Su / M / Tu / W / Th / F / Sa

__ / __ / ____

Today I Feel:

Today I'm Thankful For:

1 ______________________________

____

____

____

2 ______________________________

____

____

____

3 ______________________________

____

____

____

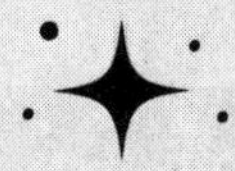

What's one small faithful thing you could do today—just like Leo did as a kid?

Write it here. Then go try it.

CALLED TO SERVE

Leo's Leap of Faith

Robert's path forward wasn't about power. It was about purpose. In his early twenties, he joined the Order of St. Augustine—a community of Catholic priests known for their simplicity, scholarship, and service.

He took a vow of poverty and committed his life to God and others. He didn't do it to be seen. He did it because it felt right. That's what a calling looks like.

Date: Su / M / Tu / W / Th / F / Sa

__ / __ / ____

Today I Feel:

Leo joined a community that helped him grow in faith, friendship, and purpose. He didn't have to do it all alone, and neither do you.

Write about one community you're a part of or one you'd like to find.

What does it feel like to belong?

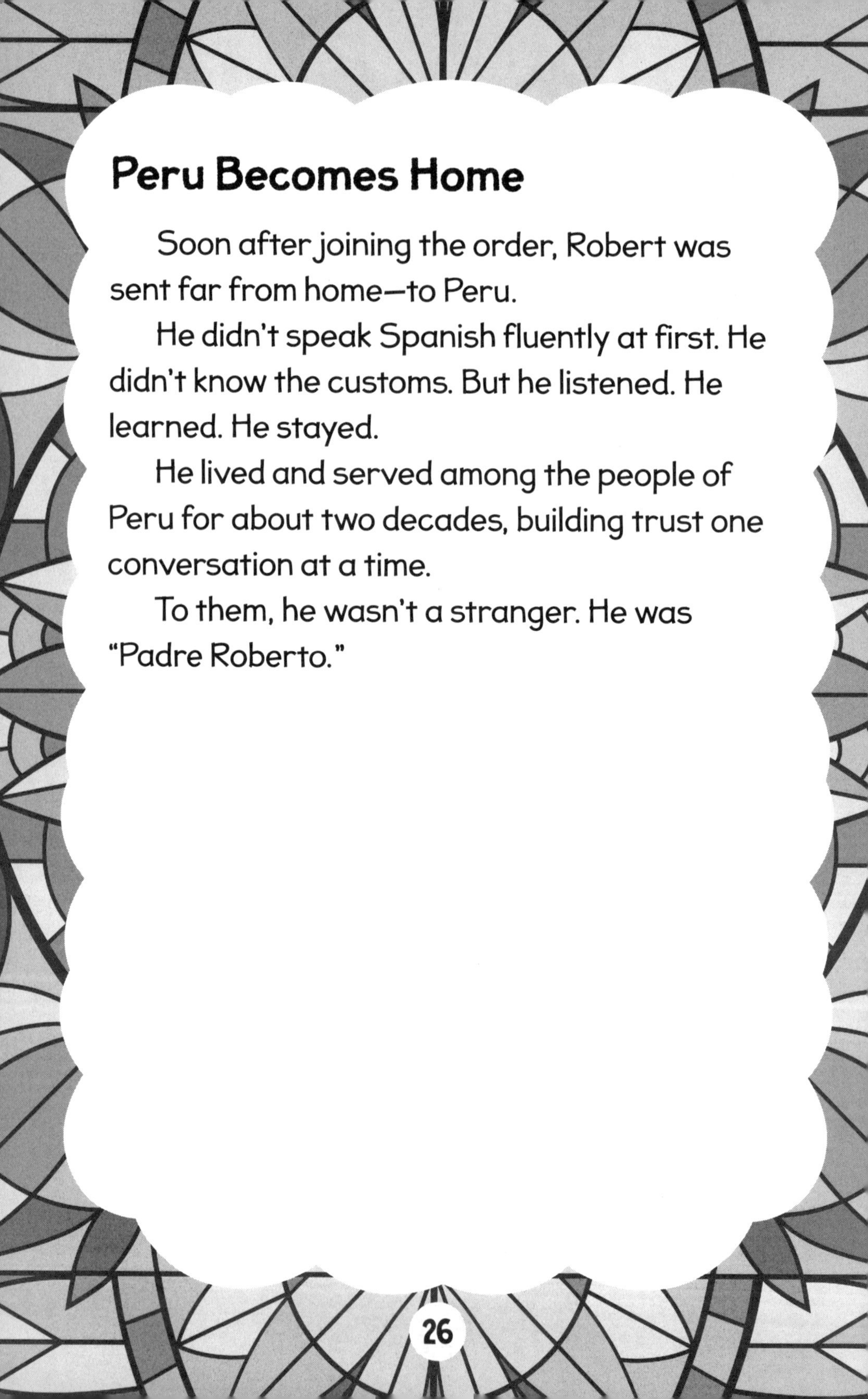

Peru Becomes Home

Soon after joining the order, Robert was sent far from home—to Peru.

He didn't speak Spanish fluently at first. He didn't know the customs. But he listened. He learned. He stayed.

He lived and served among the people of Peru for about two decades, building trust one conversation at a time.

To them, he wasn't a stranger. He was "Padre Roberto."

Date: Su / M / Tu / W / Th / F / Sa

__ / __ / ____

Today I Feel:

Today I'm Thankful For:

1 ______________________________

____

____

____

2 ______________________________

____

____

____

3 ______________________________

____

____

____

A Bishop in Work Boots

Robert's service didn't go unnoticed.

Eventually, he was named bishop of the region. But even then, Robert kept walking the dusty roads, visiting families and parishes, hearing confessions, and praying with the sick.

He didn't lead from behind a desk. He led from the streets, the homes, and the hearts of the people he served.

Date: Su / M / Tu / W / Th / F / Sa

__ / __ / ____

Today I Feel:

Think about a moment this week when you showed up even though it was hard.

What did you do? Why did it matter?

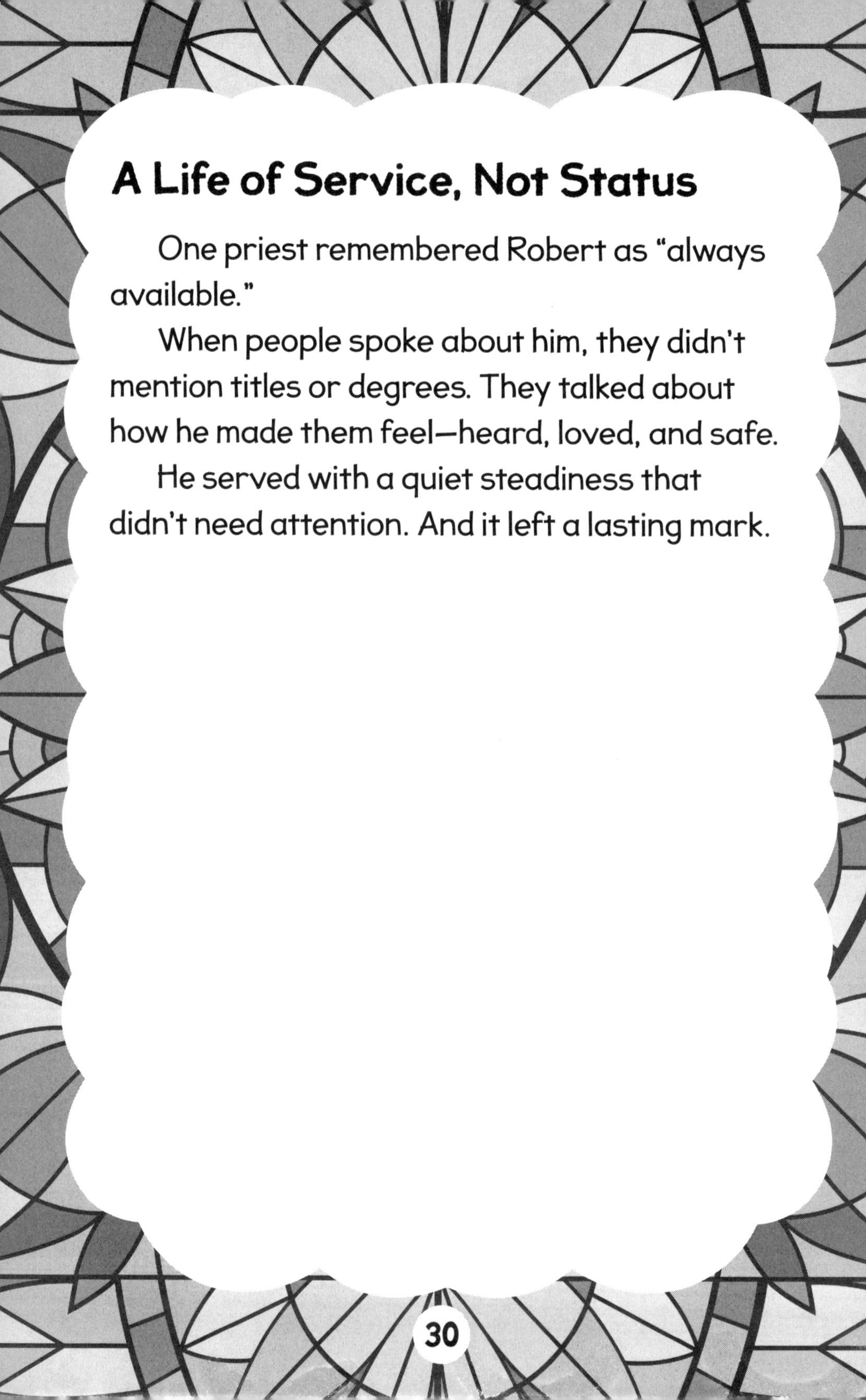

A Life of Service, Not Status

One priest remembered Robert as "always available."

When people spoke about him, they didn't mention titles or degrees. They talked about how he made them feel—heard, loved, and safe.

He served with a quiet steadiness that didn't need attention. And it left a lasting mark.

Date: Su / M / Tu / W / Th / F / Sa

__ / __ / ____

Today I Feel:

Today I'm Thankful For:

1 ______________________________

____

____

____

2 ______________________________

____

____

____

3 ______________________________

____

____

____

Leo's Lightbulbs

1 Leo lived in Peru for around twenty years.

2 He earned the affectionate nickname "Latin Yankee" for his connection to local Peruvian communities.

3 He became fluent in Spanish while living among locals.

4 He took a vow of poverty as an Augustinian priest.

5 At a church in Chulucanas, a town in Peru, he met a young altar boy named Héctor.

6 When Héctor had a daughter, named Mildred, he asked Robert to be her godfather and baptize her.

7 Years later, in 2024, Robert saw Mildred again when he returned to Chulucanas.

8 In 2023, he led relief efforts in northern Peru after a cyclone hit the area.

9 He waded through muddy floodwaters, delivered resources from his truck, and served food to those in need.

10 He was praised for uniting people from different cultures.

What Does It Mean to Serve?

Leo believed that service wasn't about being seen. It was about showing up.

What does service mean to you?

Write about a time when you helped someone without expecting anything in return.

What did you learn?

Called to Something Bigger

Leo didn't wait for a sign in the sky. He followed the nudge in his heart.

Have you ever felt pulled toward something—even something small or quiet?

Write about a moment you felt called to do the right thing.

How Can I Serve Today?

You don't have to go to another country to make a difference. Small things—kindness, presence, prayer—matter, too.

Write down three simple ways you could serve others this week.

1 ______________________________

2 ______________________________

3 ______________________________

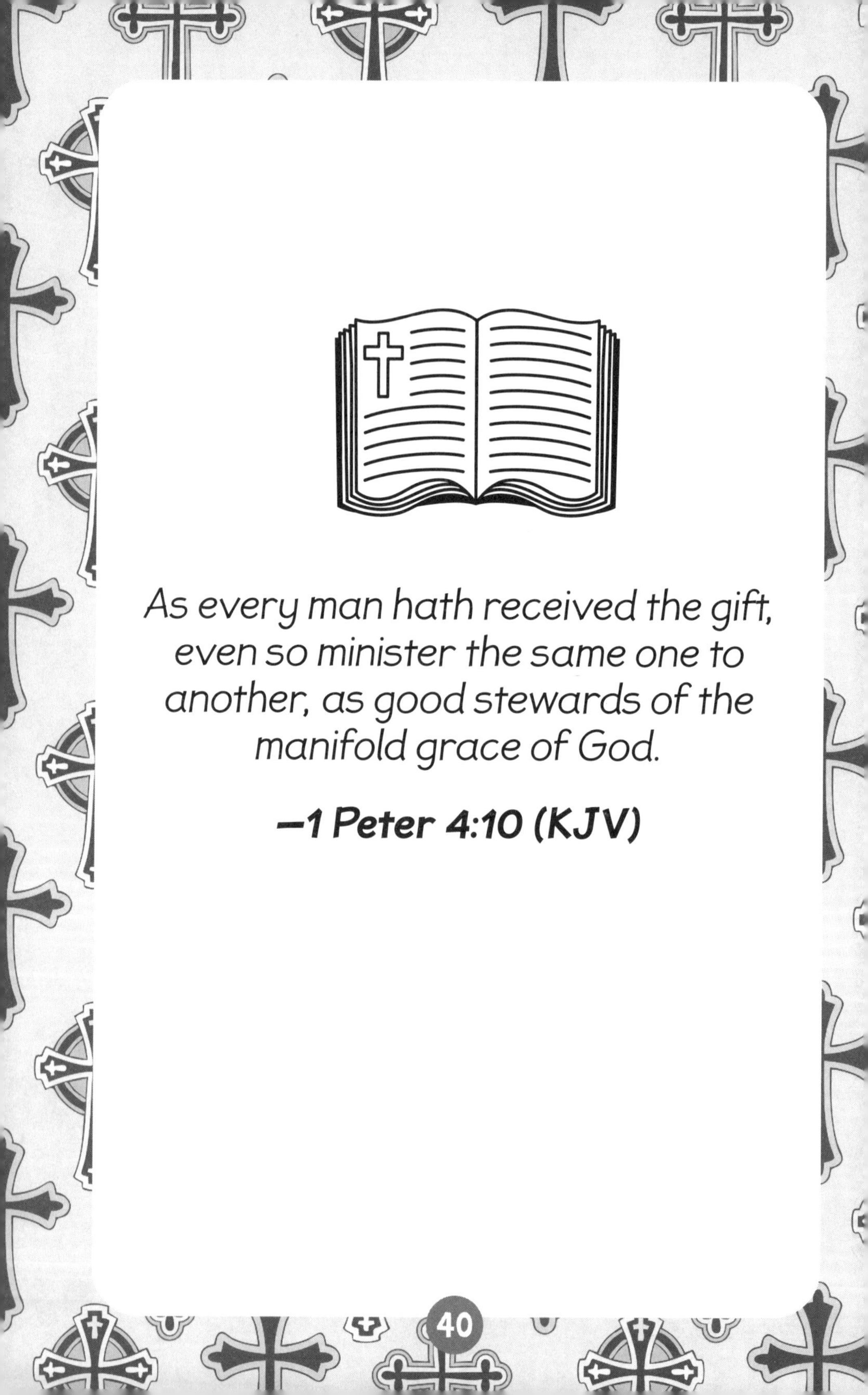

As every man hath received the gift, even so minister the same one to another, as good stewards of the manifold grace of God.

—1 Peter 4:10 (KJV)

What is one gift you've been given—kindness, creativity, courage—that you could use to serve someone else this week?

Date: Su / M / Tu / W / Th / F / Sa

__ / __ / ____

Today I Feel:

Today I'm Thankful For:

1 ____________________

2 ____________________

3 ____________________

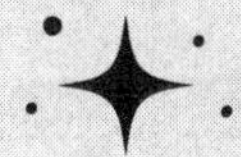

When Leo went to Peru, he didn't know the language. He didn't know the people. But he still showed up to serve. What's one new or unfamiliar place you could show up in this week with love, patience, and courage?

A GLOBAL JOURNEY

From Peru to the Vatican

Leo never expected to leave Peru. But after decades of service, his leadership caught attention far beyond the villages he walked through.

He was called to Rome to serve in the Vatican, where he helped guide bishops from around the world. He traded dirt roads for marble halls, but he stayed the same.

Even among powerful voices, Leo still listened first.

Date: Su / M / Tu / W / Th / F / Sa

__ / __ / ____

Today I Feel:

Today I'm Thankful For:

1 ______________________________

____

____

____

2 ______________________________

____

____

____

3 ______________________________

____

____

____

Building Bridges

At the Vatican, Leo worked with leaders from around the world. He spoke Spanish, English, and Italian. He often sat quietly while others debated, taking it all in.

Cardinal Timothy Dolan of New York said, "He's a citizen of the world . . . he's a bridge builder."

He didn't push. He built trust.

Date: Su / M / Tu / W / Th / F / Sa

__ / __ / ____

Today I Feel:

Leo listened more than he spoke and helped people find common ground, even when they disagreed.

Have you ever helped solve a disagreement or brought people together?

Write about a time when you were a peacemaker or helped others feel heard.

What did you learn about listening and trust?

A Reputation for Wisdom

People noticed Robert's calm. His preparation. His patience.

People who worked with Robert recall he was a great listener and "a naturally good person."

He was rarely the loudest. But he was always respected.

Date: Su / M / Tu / W / Th / F / Sa

__ / __ / ____

Today I Feel:

Today I'm Thankful For:

1 ______________________________

____

____

____

2 ______________________________

____

____

____

3 ______________________________

____

____

____

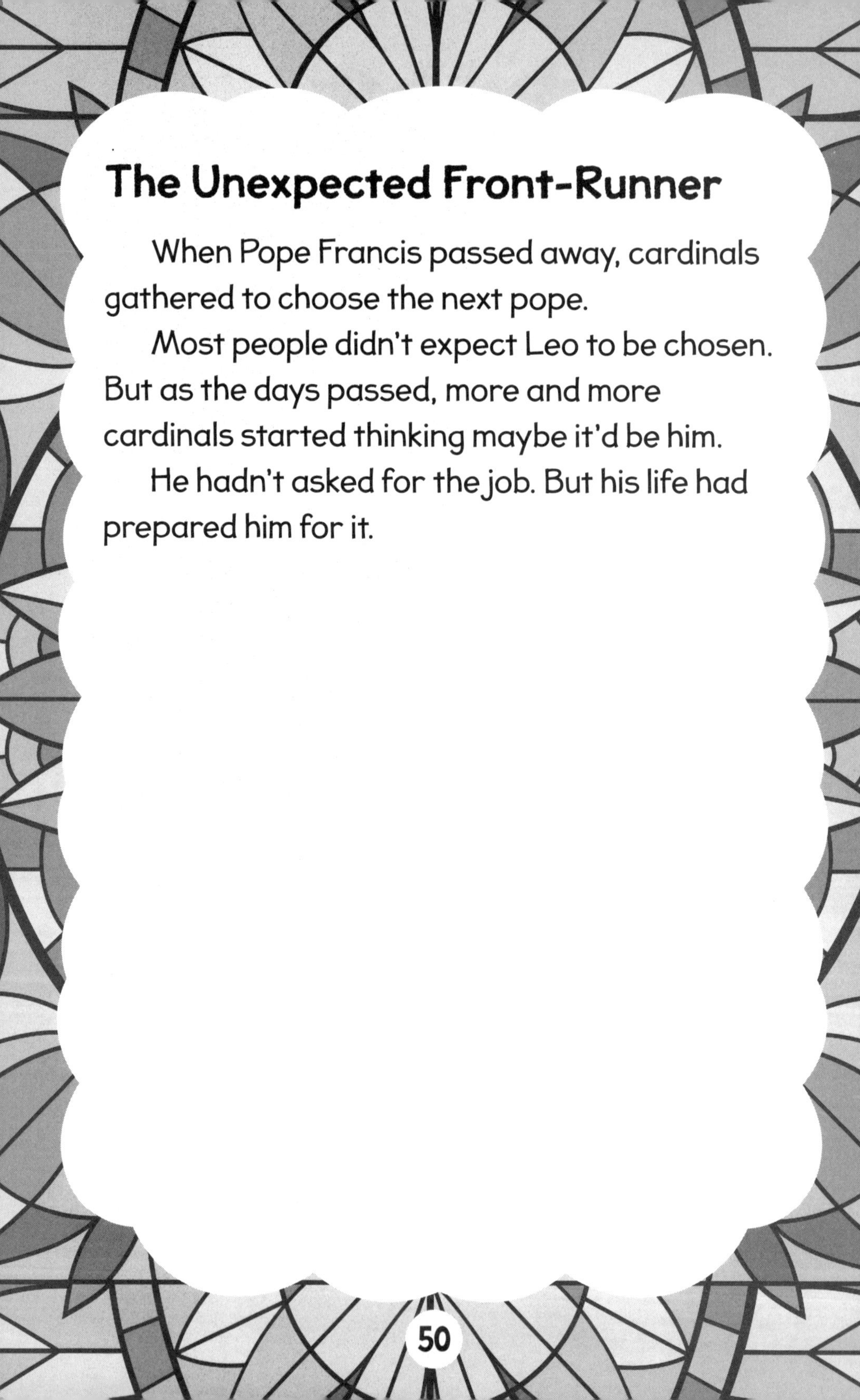

The Unexpected Front-Runner

When Pope Francis passed away, cardinals gathered to choose the next pope.

Most people didn't expect Leo to be chosen. But as the days passed, more and more cardinals started thinking maybe it'd be him.

He hadn't asked for the job. But his life had prepared him for it.

Date: Su / M / Tu / W / Th / F / Sa

__ / __ / ____

Today I Feel:

Leo didn't plan to become pope. He just kept showing up, serving others, and growing in faith. When the moment came, he was ready.

Has there ever been a moment when you were chosen for something big or surprising?

Write about a time you stepped up, even if you felt unsure at first. What helped you feel ready?

Leo's Lightbulbs

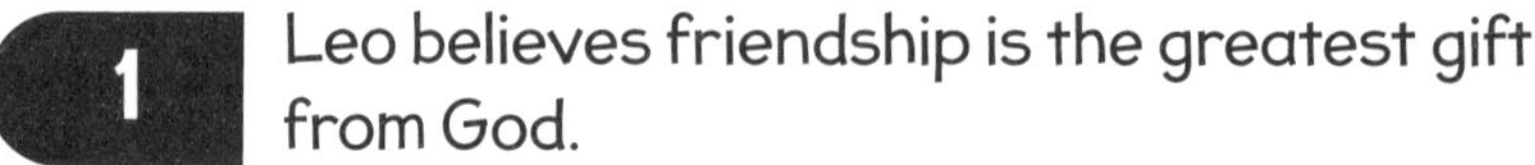

1 Leo believes friendship is the greatest gift from God.

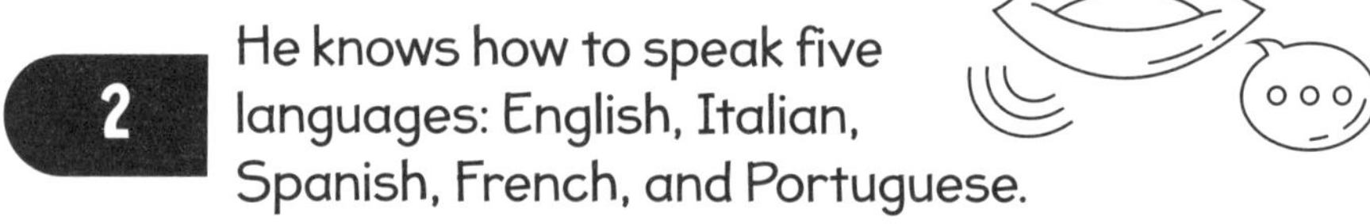

2 He knows how to speak five languages: English, Italian, Spanish, French, and Portuguese.

3 He can also read German and Latin.

4 He's a fan of tennis.

5 He wore an Apple Watch during one of his masses.

6 He has two older brothers, named Louis and John.

7 His dad was in the navy and served during World War II.

8 He likes pizza and still visits Aurelio's Pizza in Homewood, Illinois.

9 He once said in an interview, "Above all, a bishop must proclaim Jesus Christ."

10 He was the editor-in-chief of his high school yearbook.

Who Do You Trust?

Leo gained people's trust by being steady, honest, and kind.

Who do you trust?
What makes someone trustworthy in your life?
Write about a person who has earned your trust and how they did it.

Bridge Builder

Leo brought people together by listening well and seeing the good in others.

Have you ever helped two people understand each other?

Write about a time when you helped someone feel included or heard.

Quiet Confidence

Leo didn't try to impress anyone. He stayed true to who he was, and that was enough.

What's something quiet about you that is actually a strength?

Write about or draw a picture of how your calm, kindness, or stillness helps others.

*Let every man be swift to hear,
slow to speak, slow to wrath.*

—James 1:19 (KJV)

What does it mean to be "swift to hear"?

Write about how you could slow down and really listen this week—to a friend, to a parent or guardian, or even to God.

Date: Su / M / Tu / W / Th / F / Sa

__ / __ / ____

Today I Feel:

Today I'm Thankful For:

1 ______________________________

____

____

____

2 ______________________________

____

____

____

3 ______________________________

____

____

____

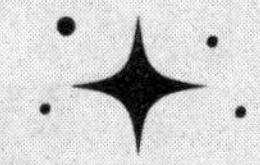

Leo showed us that the quietest person in the room can sometimes carry the most peace.

How can you carry peace in your day today?

Write about one place where you can be a calm and steady presence.

Part IV

A POPE FOR THE PEOPLE

A New Pope Is Chosen

When the conclave began, Leo was not a front-runner. Most of the world didn't even know his name.

But inside the Sistine Chapel, something unusual happened: The cardinals started to agree. The world needed unity. And Leo offered it—not with power, but with peace.

Date: **Su / M / Tu / W / Th / F / Sa**

__ / __ / ____

Today I Feel:

Leo wasn't famous. He didn't campaign or try to impress anyone. But people saw his calm, steady presence, and they trusted it.

What's one way you can lead with peace instead of power?

Write about a time when you stayed calm in a tense moment or helped bring people together by being steady and kind.

The Day the Smoke Turned White

On the day of the final vote, Leo sat quietly as the ballots were counted.

When he reached the number needed to become pope, the room erupted in applause. But Leo didn't jump up. He stayed seated, stunned.

Someone had to help him stand. The moment was sacred. And real.

Date: Su / M / Tu / W / Th / F / Sa

__ / __ / ____

Today I Feel:

Today I'm Thankful For:

1 ______________________________

____

____

____

2 ______________________________

____

____

____

3 ______________________________

____

____

____

The Humble Beginning of Pope Leo XIV

He took the name "Leo"—possibly to honor a legacy of courage and clarity—but he added his own touch: humility.

His first act was to pray: "Let us pray together for this new mission, for the whole Church, for peace in the world, and let us ask Mary, our Mother, for this special grace," he said during his first speech.

Pope Leo XIV didn't promise quick fixes. He promised to listen, to serve, and to lead with love.

Date: Su / M / Tu / W / Th / F / Sa

__ / __ / ____

Today I Feel:

Leo didn't make big promises. He started with something simple and powerful. He prayed.

If you were given a big responsibility, what's the first thing you would do?

Write about how you might lead with love. What would you pray for?

The People's Pope

Back in Chicago, people cheered. In Peru, bells rang. And across the globe, many smiled to see someone so humble step into such a powerful role.

At his inaugural mass, Pope Leo said, "I come to you as a brother, who desires to be the servant of your faith and your joy, walking with you on the path of God's love, for he wants us all to be united in one family."

Even now, Pope Leo XIV reminds the world you don't have to shout to be heard. You just have to show up and serve.

Date: Su / M / Tu / W / Th / F / Sa

__ / __ / ____

Today I Feel:

Today I'm Thankful For:

1 ______________________________

____

____

____

2 ______________________________

____

____

____

3 ______________________________

____

____

____

Leo's Lightbulbs

1. Pope Leo XIV is the first North American-born pope in history.

2. He was elected after just a few rounds of voting.

3. When elected, he was too stunned to stand.

4. Pope Leo XIV chose his name to honor an earlier pope, Leo XIII, who served from 1878 to 1903.

5. Pope Leo XIII helped protect workers and made sure they were treated fairly. Pope Leo XIV hopes to do the same thing today.

6 He still plays Wordle when he has time.

7 Pope Leo uses social media.

8 You can find him on X, formerly known as Twitter, and Instagram, where he uses the handle @pontifex.

9 He holds a mathematics degree from Villanova University.

10 He was born on a feast day, the Exaltation of the Holy Cross (September 14).

A Leader Like Leo

Leo didn't seek power. But when the world called, he answered.

What does good leadership look like to you?

Write about someone in your life who leads with kindness, courage, or calm.

How can you follow their example?

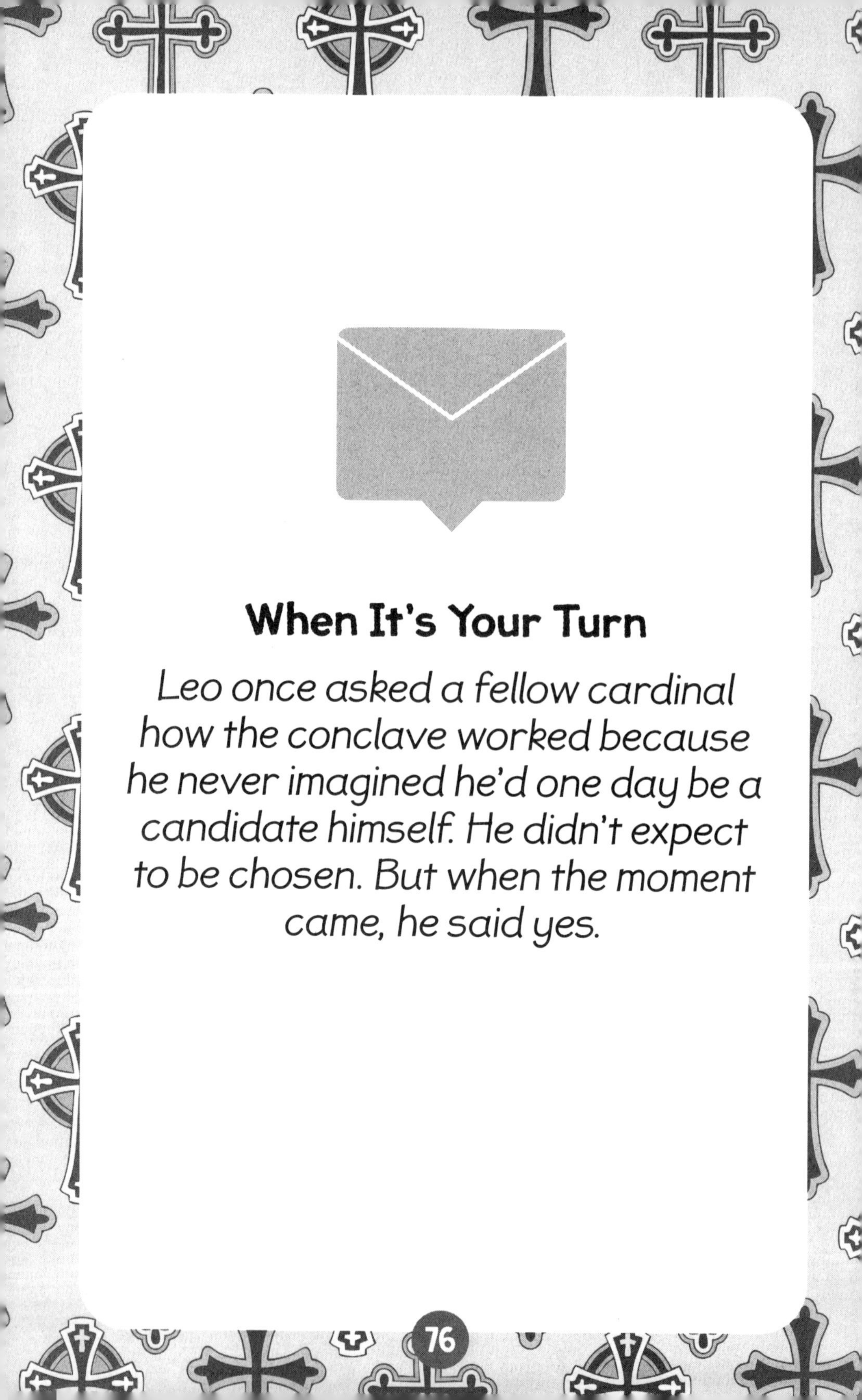

When It's Your Turn

Leo once asked a fellow cardinal how the conclave worked because he never imagined he'd one day be a candidate himself. He didn't expect to be chosen. But when the moment came, he said yes.

What's something big or new that you've said yes to?

How did it feel?

What helped you step forward?

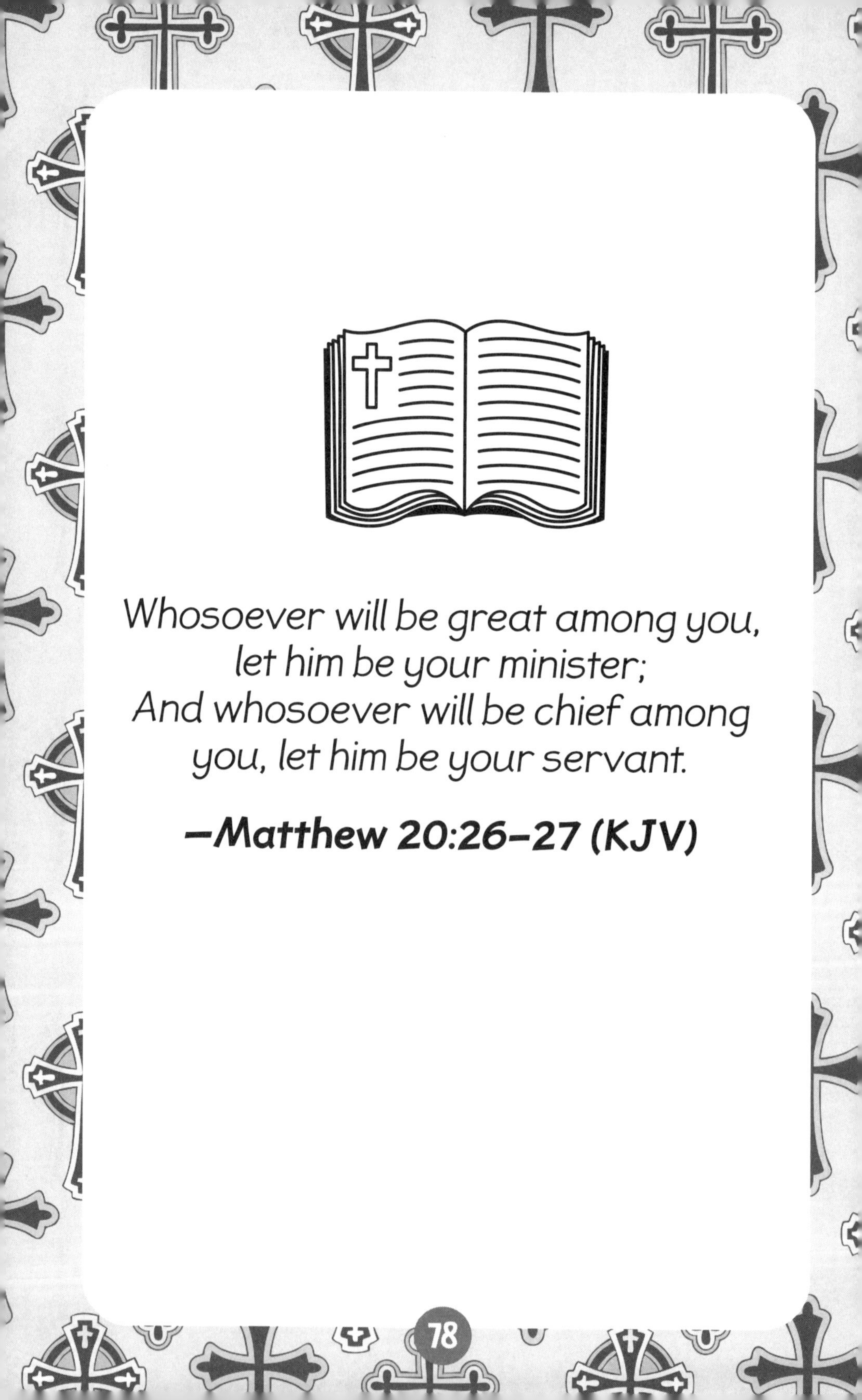

Whosoever will be great among you,
let him be your minister;
And whosoever will be chief among
you, let him be your servant.

—Matthew 20:26–27 (KJV)

What does it mean to lead by serving?

Write about one way you can be a servant-leader in your family, school, or community.

Leo never tried to become pope. He just kept showing up with love, patience, and service.

What's one way your kindness could change something small—and start something big?